# The Voyage of the Jumblies

## A Children's Play with Music

### Philip Freeman Sayer

A SAMUEL FRENCH ACTING EDITION

SAMUELFRENCH-LONDON.CO.UK
SAMUELFRENCH.COM

Copyright © 1989 by Philip Freeman Sayer
All Rights Reserved

THE VOYAGE OF THE JUMBLIES is fully protected under the copyright laws of the British Commonwealth, including Canada, the United States of America, and all other countries of the Copyright Union. All rights, including professional and amateur stage productions, recitation, lecturing, public reading, motion picture, radio broadcasting, television and the rights of translation into foreign languages are strictly reserved.

ISBN 978-0-573-05088-6

www.samuelfrench-london.co.uk

www.samuelfrench.com

### For Amateur Production Enquiries

#### United Kingdom and World excluding North America

plays@SamuelFrench-London.co.uk

020 7255 4302/01

Each title is subject to availability from Samuel French, depending upon country of performance.

CAUTION: Professional and amateur producers are hereby warned that THE VOYAGE OF THE JUMBLIES is subject to a licensing fee. Publication of this play does not imply availability for performance. Both amateurs and professionals considering a production are strongly advised to apply to the appropriate agent before starting rehearsals, advertising, or booking a theatre. A licensing fee must be paid whether the title is presented for charity or gain and whether or not admission is charged.

The professional rights in this play are controlled by Samuel French Ltd, 52 Fitzroy Street, London, W1T 5JR.

No one shall make any changes in this title for the purpose of production. No part of this book may be reproduced, stored in a retrieval system, or transmitted in any form, by any means, now known or yet to be invented, including mechanical, electronic, photocopying, recording, videotaping, or otherwise, without the prior written permission of the publisher. No one shall upload this title, or part of this title, to any social media websites.

The right of Philip Freeman Sayer to be identified as author of this work has been asserted by him in accordance with Section 77 of the Copyright, Designs and Patents Act 1988

## THE VOYAGE OF THE JUMBLIES

First presented by Stage '65 Youth Theatre at Salisbury Playhouse, Salisbury, on 14th June, 1988, with the following cast:

| | |
|---|---|
| **Narrators** | Katherine Armfelt, Emma Coryndon, Polly Reeve-Tucker |
| **1st Reciter/Father Jumbly** | Barnaby Meats |
| **2nd Reciter/Mother Jumbly** | Katy Bray |
| **3rd Reciter/Jumbly Maid** | Lotte Elwell |
| **4th Reciter/Jum** | Jonathan Donovan |
| **Objector/Quangle Wangle** | Emma Stewart |
| **Pobble** | Neil Coombes |
| **Aunt Jobiska** | Laura Vincent |
| **Mrs Canary** | Zoë Rawlence |
| **Mr Canary** | Edward Collier |
| **Pelican King** | Andrew Docherty |
| **Dong** | Thomas Docherty |
| **Turkey** | Edward Cheesman |
| **Owl** | Jackson Baird |
| **Pussy-cat** | Daruni Jones |
| **Piggy-wig** | Mark Gilchrist |
| **Fimble Fowl** | Charles Woodford |
| **Jumbly Woman** | Charlotte Mason |
| **Jumbly Child** | Rose Easton |

Other parts were played by Gabriela Blandy, Freya Stewart, Laura Bartlett, Fiona Verdon-Smith, Lucy Edgar, Zoë Bishop and Adam Pelly.

With Adrian Ferry (flute, drums), Adam Longlands (piano, bass), Stephen White (guitar)

Directed by Lynn Wyfe
Designed by David Mauchline
Choreographed by Felicity Camm

## CHARACTERS

**Narrator**
**1st Reciter/Father,** a Jumbly
**2nd Reciter/Mother,** his wife
**3rd Reciter/Jumbly Maid,** their daughter
**4th Reciter/Jum,** their young son
**Objector/Quangle Wangle**
**Pobble**
**Aunt Jobiska,** the Pobble's Aunt
**Pelican King**
**Dong**
**Turkey**
**Owl**
**Pussy-cat**
**Piggy-wig**
**Mr Canary**
**Mrs Canary**
**Fimble Fowl**
**Jumbly Woman**
**Jumbly Child**

Other **Jumblies** (at least five), **Pelicans** (about five) **Quangle Wangle's Retinue (Snake, Bumble-bee, Frog, Blue Baboon, Orient Calf, Attery Squash, Bisky Bat)**

Some parts may be doubled if there are not enough players. The part of the Narrator is a large one, and may be split between two or more actors.

## PRODUCTION NOTES

**Staging**
Although *The Voyage of the Jumblies* could be performed equally well on a conventional proscenium stage, the play was really devised with an arena style presentation in mind. The advantage of this type of staging with a young cast is that you tend to get a more natural and intimate, less stagey performance, and it also brings the audience closer to the performers, which helps with audibility. It was important to keep everything as flexible as possible so that it could be adapted to any shape of arena. For this reason the location of individual entrances and exits are not specified in the script. There are no scenes as such, the action being continuous, flowing from one time and place to the next.

*No scenery is necessary*, although a few rostra might come in handy to vary the levels. However, a set *was* used in the first production at Salisbury Playhouse and I include the following notes and a ground plan which the producer may find useful.

The play was performed on a deep thrust stage (see ground plan on page viii) backed by a huge, hinged book with the title on the cover. During the course of the action this was opened or closed by members of the cast to vary the background, and from it emerged some of the characters and props. When open it showed the "Far and Few" rhyme opposite a painting of a pounding sea. A large hole in this served as an entrance. Other entrances were from behind the tree and the bush, and mainly (but not exclusively) the Jumbly characters entered from the bush end while the others— Pobble, Dong, Owl and Pussy-cat, Pelicans etc.—came from the tree. The other principal element was a clump of toadstools on which the Narrators sat when not speaking. (Although there is only one Narrator in the script, it was decided to split this large part between three actors.)

Movable waves were operated by the actors when the Jumbly family started their journey, and the rest of the set was dressed with driftwood, lobster pots, rocks and polystyrene oysters to continue the maritime theme. The waves and the tree were cut-outs and everything brightly painted to give a storybook feel, and the floor was washed blue-green to represent land or sea as the action demanded. A large sieve was made on a wooden framework covered with chicken wire, then scrimmed with cloth and glue and painted. The Crumpetty Tree was made in the same way, and they were both brought on by members of the cast when required.

**Costume**
All the cast wore large T-shirts and footless tights dyed in various colours appropriate to their characters, which were further differentiated by masks, wigs, beaks or feet. These were all kept fairly simple, not to overburden or overshadow the actors. The way the characters move is the best way to show who they are, and these costumes gave them the necessary freedom of movement.

It is important that the Jumblies' heads should *not* be green (and is mentioned in the text). I feel that green masks or make-up would be too crude and take away the subtlety of expression of the principal characters. In fact even with the smaller parts full masks are better avoided as they reduce both expression and audibility, particularly with young actors.

The Pelicans' beaks were carved from expanded polystyrene and then coated with muslin and PVA glue before painting. Cloth straps and velcro probably hold them better than elastic. The Pelicans also had large webbed feet, made from foam rubber stuck on to old plimsoles. The Pobble's feet were made in the same way, with detachable toes held on with velcro!

The Dong was dressed in black, and had a large red nose which he put on towards the end of Act I. This was translucent and contained a torch bulb, battery and switch. It looked very effective as he searched for his friends in the dark. The Quangle Wangle's hat was a large sombrero type extended to make it as wide as possible, and covered with odd scraps of material, lace, etc.

**Props**
Almost none of the items mentioned in the text need actually appear — even the sieve could be represented by a pool of light. Good use of mime can imply the existence of objects without the problems of where to produce them from and where to put them when you've finished with them, which can hold up the action. I leave it to the individual producer to decide how much physical

reality is wanted, while keeping the action as fluid as possible. However, I do think that the wrapper of scarlet flannel, being central to the plot, *should* appear.

**Music**

The music for the songs is on pages 35–43. The tunes, which I have adapted from traditional folk songs, are included as suggested melodies only. Those more accomplished muscially than I am should not be deterred from making their own settings and arrangements.

I am grateful to Lynn Wyfe and David Mauchline for their help in the preparation of these notes.

Philip Freeman Sayer

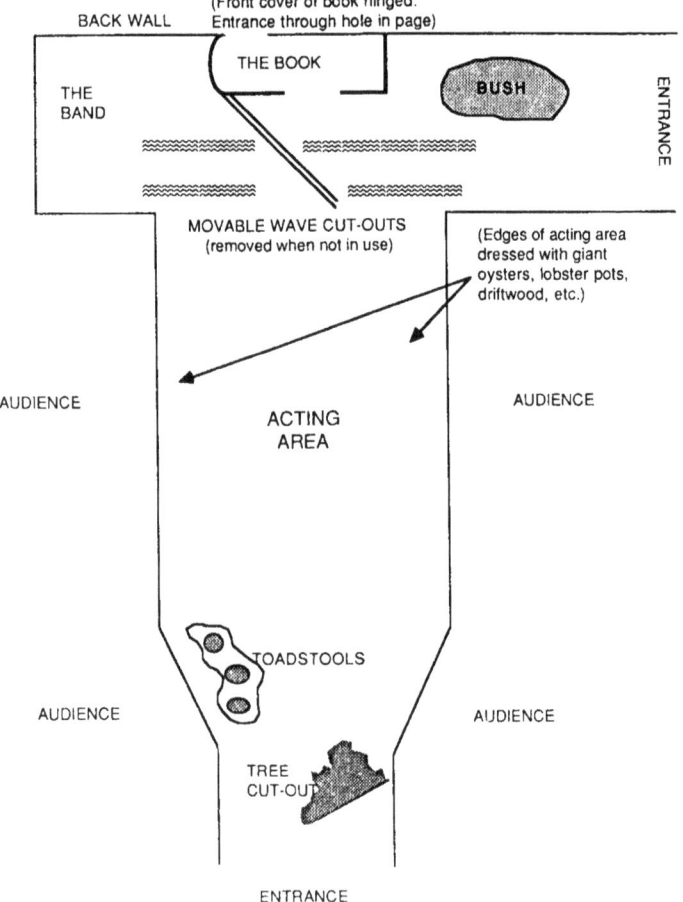

**SONGS**

The Coast of Coromandel
Calico Pie
The Pelican Chorus
The Owl and the Pussy-Cat
Far and Few

The music for these songs is given on pages 35–43.

## ACT I

*The Narrator and four Reciters enter and stand in best "school recitation" manner*

**Narrator** Ladies and Gentlemen, "The Jumblies" by Edward Lear.
**All** Far and few, far and few,
Are the lands where the Jumblies live;
Their heads are green, and their hands are blue,
And they went to sea in a Sieve.
**Narrator** They went to sea in a Sieve, they did,
In a Sieve they went to sea:
**1st Reciter** In spite of all their friends could say,
On a winter's morn, on a stormy day,
In a Sieve they went to sea!
**2nd Reciter** And when the Sieve turned round and round,
And everyone cried,
**3rd Reciter** "You'll all be drowned!"
**2nd Reciter** They called out aloud,
**4th Reciter** "Our Sieve ain't big,
But we don't care a button! we don't care a fig!
In a Sieve we'll go to sea!"
**All** Far and few, far and few
Are the lands where the Jumblies live;
Their heads are green, and their hands are blue,
And they went to sea in a Sieve.
**Objector** (*from the audience*) Why?
**All** (*horrified at the interruption*) What?
**Objector** (*standing*) Not what—why? It all sounds highly unlikely to me!
**Narrator** It's a poem.
**Objector** Yes, but what's it all about? Who are these Jumblies? Why did they go to sea?
**1st Reciter** Perhaps they were seeking their fortunes——
**2nd Reciter** —or beautiful lands——
**3rd Reciter** —finding new friends——

**4th Reciter** — or just an adventure!
**Objector** But why in a Sieve?
**Narrator** Why not? And anyway, you're all wrong. It was like this: (*story-telling voice*) "Once upon a time on the rocky shores of Coromandel lived the Jumblies. They were a happy people, and spent most of their time paddling in the warm waters and fishing for their suppers ..."
**Objector** Fish suppers!
**Narrator** No, oblong oysters, which they caught with a Sieve.
**Objector** Huh! I thought you'd work that Sieve into it, somehow!
**Narrator** To continue: thus they passed the happy hours on the coasts of Coromandel.

*Coromandel*

*All the Jumblies go about their daily tasks, including the Four Reciters, who now take on their Jumbly roles — as they all sing*

### Song: The Coast of Coromandel

**Jumblies**     On the coast of Coromandel
On the impecunious sand,
There the Jumblies dance and dandle
As they gambol hand in hand.
All along the shores they leap,
Where the oblong oysters creep,
And go fishing in the deep
Till it's time to go to sleep.

A large Sieve without a handle
They employ without delay
On that coast of Coromandel
Where the Bong-trees softly sway;
Crooning songs evocative
To the oysters where they live
While they catch them in the Sieve,
Gently catch them in the Sieve.

On the coast of Coromandel
Next the superincumbent sea,
By the light of half a candle
They prepare to cook their tea—

Act I 3

>      And the oblong oysters roast
>      With a slice of scroobious toast
>      On that Coromandel coast,
>      Dreamy Coromandel coast.

*They dance*

*The Jumblies exit dancing, leaving Jum*

**Narrator** Now there was one cheeky young Jumbly who was always wandering off on his own. His name was—er, Jum ...
**Objector** (*scornfully*) Jum!
**Narrator** Yes—Jum, and he lived with his mother and——
**Objector** Just a minute—why haven't they got green heads? It particularly said that their heads were green.
**Narrator** Well, you can't believe everything you hear.
**Objector** Just as I thought; a lot of nonsense from beginning to end! But since we've got this far, we *might* as well hear the rest. (*He sits*)
**Narrator** Thank you. Jum lived with his mother and his father and his sister, the Jumbly Maid. And one day ...

*Mother and Jumbly Maid enter*

**Mother** Jum! Where are you off to?
**Jum** Just going for a walk.
**Mother** I know your walks. Don't go too far—we'll be having supper as soon as Father comes home.
**Jum** Yes, Mum.
**Jumbly Maid** Don't worry, Jum—I might leave you a *few* oysters.

*Mother and Jumbly Maid exit*

**Jum** Oysters again! It's the same every day. Catch oysters, cook oysters, eat oysters and dance on the sand till it's time to go to bed. I wish one day something different would happen.

*A cry is heard, like an animal in pain*

Whatever was that? Something's hurt. I'd better have a look. Wait a minute, though—supposing this something is being attacked by another something. Or several somethings!

>      There was an old man who screamed out
>      Whenever they knocked him about;

> So they took off his boots, and fed him with fruits,
> And continued to knock him about.

I don't want them to knock me about! I'd better not go.

*The cry is heard again*

No, I must go—it might need my help, whatever it is. Hang on, I'm coming!

*Pobble enters*

(*Finding Pobble*) Why, it's a young creature! What's the matter, little fellow, are you hurt?

*Pobble makes whimpering noises*

Don't worry, I'll help you. Come on, don't be frightened. I'll take you to my father—he'll know what to do.

**Narrator** So Jum helped the little creature back to the village, and before long all the Jumblies were crowding round, anxious to see what was wrong.

*Father, Mother, Jumbly Maid and other Jumblies enter*

**Father** Now stand back everyone. My son's young friend is going to tell me all about himself, but I can't hear what he says if you all chatter on so. Now, little fellow——

**1st Jumbly** Who is he?

**2nd Jumbly** What is he?

*Pobble speaks indistinctly through his crying. Father listens closely*

**Father** He says he's a Pobble—so he pobble-by is! That's just my little joke, you understand.

*The others groan*

Now, young Pobble, what's the matter? Speak up, we shan't hurt you.

**Pobble** I've lost—(*he sniffs*)—I've lost . . .

**1st Jumbly** He's lost his way——

**2nd Jumbly** He's lost his friends——

**3rd Jumbly** He's lost his handkerchief——

**4th Jumbly** He's lost his memory——

**5th Jumbly** He's lost *all hope*!

# Act I

**All** What has he lost?
**Pobble** I've lost my TOES!
**All** Toes?
**Father** But look here now, you can't have lost your toes just like that! I mean--where did you last have them?
**Pobble** On my feet!
**Father** Yes--well of course, I know that. But where were you?
**Pobble** I was swimming across the Bristol Channel, (*he sniffs*) and when I got out, they'd all gone!
**Father** Gone? When you were swimming the Channel? But are you sure you had toes when you set out?
**Pobble** Yes--lots of toes. Lots and lots.

*The Jumblies scatter to look for the toes, murmuring "Lots of toes—but where can they be?" and so on, leaving one to act as Aunt Jobiska in the following flashback sequence*

| | |
|---|---|
| **Narrator** | The Pobble who has no toes |
| | Had once as many as we; |
| | When they said, "Some day you may lose them all" |
| | He replied: |
| **Pobble** | Fish fiddle de-dee! |
| **Narrator** | And his Aunt Jobiska make him drink |
| | Lavender water tinged with pink, |
| | For she said |
| **Aunt Jobiska** | The World in general knows |
| | There's nothing so good for a Pobble's toes! |
| **Narrator** | The Pobble who has no toes |
| | Swam across the Bristol Channel; |
| | But before he set out he wrapped his nose |
| | In a piece of scarlet flannel. |
| | For his Aunt Jobiska said: |

*She ties the wrapper round Pobble's nose*

**Aunt Jobiska** No harm
Can come to his toes if his nose is warm,
And it's perfectly known that a Pobble's toes
Are safe - provided he minds his nose.

*Pobble starts to swim*

**Narrator**   The Pobble swam fast and well,
And when boats or ships came near him
He tinkledy-binkledy-winkled a bell
So that all the world could hear him.

*Mrs Canary flies in*

But before he touched the shore,
The shore of the Bristol Channel,
A bright young Birdling carried away
His wrapper of scarlet flannel.

*Mrs Canary exits with the wrapper*

And when he came to observe his feet,
Formerly garnished with toes so neat,
His face at once became forlorn
On perceiving that all of his toes were——

**Pobble**   GORN!

**Jum** All of them?

**Pobble** Every single one! And I've never seen them since. (*He sniffs*) I'm lonely and lost, and I want my tea and I want my Teddy and I WANT MY TOES! (*He howls*)

**Father** Yes, yes. There, there, little fellow, don't take on so. We're all very sorry for you, of course, but there's really nothing we can do.

**Jum** Yes, there is! We could try to get his toes back.

**Father** But how? It's impossible—we wouldn't know where to start.

**Mother** It's a kind thought, Jum, but I can't really see that we could help.

**Jum** Why not? Look, if his toes disappeared when he lost his wrapper of scarlet flannel, then all we have to do is to find it and his toes will come back!

**Father** Ridiculous! Preposterous! I've never heard anything like it in all my born days!

**Jumbly Maid** I agree with Jum—we must try.

**Father** You too, Jumbly Maid? I give up. Mother, try to talk some sense into your children.

**Mother** I'm not sure, dear, perhaps they're right; we really ought to try.

**Father** Have you all gone mad? And where do you suggest we look for this scarlet wrapper?

## Act I

**Jum** At sea. He lost it at sea, so that's where we'll search.
**Father** At sea? And what are we going to use as a boat, may I ask? Or do you expect us all to swim?
**Jum** The Sieve! We'll go to sea in the Sieve!
**1st Jumbly** Did you hear that? They're going to sea in a Sieve!
**2nd Jumbly** They'll get wet——
**3rd Jumbly** They'll get hungry——
**4th Jumbly** They'll catch fish——
**5th Jumbly** They'll catch flu!
**1st Jumbly** But a Sieve! They're going to sea in a Sieve!

*The Jumbly family load the Sieve—which could be a large hoop or simply a pool of light—while the others get into position for waving them off, as they all chant*

**All**  Far and few, far and few,
Are the lands where the Jumblies live;
Their heads are green, and their hands are blue,
And they went to sea in a Sieve.

*Repeat as necessary*

**Father** Fellow Jumblies! As soon as we have provisioned our— our *vessel*, we will be leaving you on our great adventure; to go where no Jumbly has ever gone before. Who knows what may be waiting for us on the other side of that wild impetuous sea, as we desperately seek for that vital piece of scarlet flannel which even now may be——
**Jum** Get on with it, Dad!
**Father** What? Oh yes. Well, now to finish loading the boat——er, Sieve.
So far we have a useful cart,
And a pound of rice, and a cranberry tart
And a hive of silvery bees.
**Mother**  And we'll need a pig——
**Jumbly Maid**  And some green Jackdaws——
**Jum**  And a lovely monkey with lollipop paws!
**Father**  Don't be silly, Jum. And thirty—no, forty, bottles
Of Ring-Bo-Ree, and no end of Stilton cheese.
**Mother**  I don't think we've got room for much more.
**Father** We'll forget the pig and the Jackdaws, then, but we mustn't forget the Ring-Bo-Ree. Now I'm not one to make a speech, but on an occasion like this——

**Jum**  Get in, Dad!
**Father**  Oh, very well. To sea, then—to sea in a Sieve!
**Jumblies**  Hooray!

*The other Jumblies wave them off and exit backwards as if the Sieve were moving, and their voices die away as they chant*

> Far and few, far and few,
> Are the lands where the Jumblies live;
> Their heads are green, and their hands are blue,
> And they went to sea in a Sieve.

*The other Jumblies exit, leaving the Sieve and its occupants*

**Narrator**   They sailed away in a Sieve, they did,
   In a Sieve they sailed so fast,
   With only a beautiful pea-green veil
   Tied with a riband by way of a sail,
   To a small tobacco-pipe mast;
   And every one said, who saw them go,
   "Oh won't they soon be upset, you know!
   For the sky is dark, and the voyage is long,
   And happen what may, it's extremely wrong
   In a Sieve to sail so fast!"

**Objector**  (*jumping up*) You're not kidding! I've never heard a more stupid story in my life! I'm not listening to any more of this. (*Going towards the exit*) To sea in a Sieve, indeed—what a ridiculous idea; the water would come in!

*The Objector exits*

**Narrator**   You're quite right—it did.
   The water it soon came in, it did,
   The water it soon came in;
   So to keep them dry, they wrapped their feet
   In a pinky paper all folded neat,
   And they fastened it down with a pin.
   And they passed the night in a crockery-jar,
   And each of them said "How wise we are!
   Though the sky be dark, and the voyage be long,
   Yet we never can think we were rash or wrong
   While round in our Sieve we spin!"

Act I

**Jum** Dad, this pinky paper's not really working. Mine's gone all soggy and squodging to my feet.
**Jumbly Maid** Well, mine is all right.
**Jum** But you're nice and snug in the crockery-jar. There's not enough room for me and my legs are sticking out.
**Mother** Now stop arguing, you two. It *is* a bit damp but we'll just have to make the best of it. If you like, I'll sing you a lullaby.
**Jum** Ooh, yes!
**Jumbly Maid** Sing Calico Pie, Mother.
**Father** Good idea, Jumbly Maid. I will accompany on my gong.
**Jum** Oh, no!
        There was an old man with a gong,
        Who bashed at it all the day long;
        But they called out "O law, you're a horrid old bore",
        So they smashed that old man with his gong!
**Mother** Jum!
**Jum** Sorry, Mum.
**Father** Yes, well—perhaps I'll save the gong until later. Do sing, dear.

*Mother sings and the others sleepily join in the chorus, until only Mother and Jum are left awake. During the song, puppets of birds and fish could circle the Sieve. The tune should be a quiet lullaby, rather wistful*

### Song: Calico Pie

**Mother**    Calico Pie
        The little birds fly,
        Down to the Calico Tree——
        Their wings were blue,
        And they sang "Tilly-Loo"
        Till away they flew
        And they never came back to me.

        (*Chorus*)    They never came back
                       They never came back——
                       They never came back to me.

Calico Jam,
The little fish swam
Down to the Calico Sea———
He took off his hat
To the sole and the sprat,
And the Willeby-wat,
But they never came back to me.

(*Chorus*)   They never came back
They never came back———
They never came back to me.

**Jum**  Mum, why did they never come back?
**Mother**  I don't know, dear—lots of things never come back; the lost days of childhood, a rose first breaking from the bud.
**Jum**  But we'll come back one day, won't we?
**Mother**  Of course we will, dear, when we've found the scarlet flannel.
**Jum**  And the Pobble's toes—they'll come back. They will, won't they, Mum?
**Mother**  I certainly hope so, Jum—I certainly hope so. (*She continues to hum the tune quietly while the Narrator speaks*)
**Narrator**   And all night long they sailed away,
And when the sun went down
They whistled and warbled a moony song
To the echoing sound of a coppery gong,
In the shade of the mountains brown.
"O Timballoo! How happy we are,
When we live in a Sieve and a crockery-jar,
And all night long in the moonlight pale
We sail away with a pea-green sail,
In the shade of the mountains brown."
**Jumbly Maid**  Oh!
**Mother**  What was that?
**Jumbly Maid**  I don't know—there was a sort of bump.
**Jum**  We've hit something.
**Father**  Don't be silly, Jum, it's not possible—what is there to hit?
**Mother**  We're not moving.
**Father**  Not moving? Good heavens, you're right—we're aground!
**Jum**   There was an old man in a boat
Who said "I'm afloat, I'm afloat!"

# Act I

When they said "No you ain't", he was ready to faint—
That unhappy old man in a boat!

**Father** Unhappy! Why, I'm delighted that we've reached land at last, wherever it may be. Come on!

*They disembark*

**Jum** Look—oysters!

**Mother** And those hills; surely they're the same hills that we see from home.

**Father** The Chankly Bore? It certainly looks like it.

**Jumbly Maid** Perhaps we've gone round in a circle and landed back in Coromandel.

**Father** I don't think so. They look like the same hills, but there's something different about them. For one thing they're on the wrong side; they ought to be over there.

**Jum** No, it's us.

**Father** Whatever do you mean?

**Jum** *We're* on the wrong side. I mean, those are the hills of the Chankly Bore, but we're looking at the other side of them.

**Mother** Then where are we?

**Father** No Jumbly has ever crossed that Range, but I've heard that beyond lies the Great Gromboolian Plain, an awful place. We could be in great peril!

**Jum** Dad, someone's coming!

**Father** Hide, all of you, quickly!

*The Pelican King enters with other Pelicans, and they do a jerky, strutting dance as they sing*

### Song: The Pelican Chorus

**Pelicans**  Ploffskin, Pluffskin, Pelican Jee!
We think no birds so happy as we!
Plumpskin, Ploshkin, Pelican Jill——
We think so then and we thought so still!

We live on the Nile. The Nile we love.
By night we sleep on the cliffs above;
By day we fish, and at eve we stand
On long bare islands of yellow sand,
*(Speaking as an echo)*
(Sand, sand, sand, sand)

(*Chorus*)

And when the sun sinks slowly down
And the great rock walls grown dark and brown,
The purple river rolls fast and dim
And the ivory ibis starlike skim,
(*Speaking as an echo*)
(Skim, skim, skim, skim)

(*Chorus*)

Then wing to wing we dance around
Stamping our feet with a flumpy sound,
Clashing our beaks as Pelicans ought,
And this is the song we nightly snort,
(*Speaking as an echo*)
(Snort, snort, snort, snort)

(*Chorus*)

**Pelican King** Ploffskin, Pluffskin, what have we here?
**Pelicans** (*severally, as an echo*) Here, here, here, here, here!
**Father** Good-evening to you. We are harmless travellers. Our Sieve ran aground here and we are lost. May we enquire where we are?
**Pelican King** Ploffskin, Pluffskin, indeed you may!
**Pelicans** (*as before*) May, may, may, may, may!
**Pelican King** This is the Zemmery Fidd, on the very edge of the Great Gromboolian Plain. No-one lives here, apart from—but we'd rather not mention that.
**Father** So you . . .?
**Pelican King** I am the Pelican King, and these are my subjects. We live by the banks of the Nile and come here merely to feed on the oblong oysters. We are going now, and I advise you to leave as soon as you can.
**Pelicans** Can, can, can, can, can!
**Father** But why?
**Mother** Why?
**Jumbly Maid** Why?
**Jum** Why?

*The Jumblies sound like the Pelicans, and Father glares at them*

**Father** Yes, why?
**Pelican King** Why? Ploffskin, Pluffskin, because of the Dong!
**Pelicans** (*like bells*) Dong, dong, dong, dong, dong!
**Father** Stop; you're making my head ring! What are you talking about?
**Pelican King**  When awful darkness and silence reign
    Over the Great Gromboolian Plain,
    The wandering Dong through the forest goes ...
**Father** The Dong?
**Mother** What Dong?
**Jumbly Maid** What *is* a Dong?
**Pelican King** Who knows?
**Pelicans** Knows, knows, knows, knows, knows!
**Pelican King** But I shouldn't stay here to find if I were you, Goodbye!
**Pelicans** Bye, bye, bye, bye, bye!

*The Pelicans exit to Pelican music*

**Father** Well, what strange creatures! But perhaps we should take their advice.
**Jum** Oh no, not back in the Sieve—just when I'd got used to standing up.
**Mother** And we really ought to catch some oysters while we're here.
**Father** But what of the Dong?
**Jum** I don't believe there *is* a Dong.

*A moan is heard, off*

  Well, perhaps I do a bit!
**Father** Back to the Sieve, quick!

*Dong enters and chases them*

**Dong** Come back!

*Jumbly Maid trips and is caught*

  *The other Jumblies escape*

**Jumbly Maid** Let me go! Please don't hurt me!
**Dong** I won't hurt you. I wouldn't hurt anyone.
**Jumbly Maid** Then please let me go.
**Dong** But you might run away.

**Jumbly Maid** If I promise not to run away, will you let me go?
**Dong** All right, but you must keep your promise. (*He releases her*)
**Jumbly Maid** Was that you moaning just now?
**Dong** Yes. I'm the Dong, and I live here on my own—*all* on my own.
**Jumbly Maid** Aren't you lonely?
**Dong** What do *you* think?
**Jumbly Maid** Is that why you don't want me to run away?

*He nods sadly*

Just a minute. (*She walks away*)
**Dong** You promised!
**Jumbly Maid** I'm not going away, silly; I'm just going to call my family. (*Calling*) It's all right—I've found a friend!
**Dong** (*pleased*) Friend!

*The other Jumblies enter*

**Jumbly Maid** This is the Dong.
**Father** Very pleased to meet you, Mr Dong. We are the Jumbly family—this is our son, Jum. Sit down and share some oysters with us, and we'll tell you all about our adventures.

*They sit*

You see, it all started when we found the Pobble——
**Jum** *I* found the Pobble.
**Father** Quite; Jum found the Pobble, and then—but we'd better explain more about ourselves. We live on the coast of Coromandel and . . .

*Father's voice fades away and the friendly converation between them all continues in dumb-show while the Narrator speaks*

**Narrator**  For the first time in years
      The Dong was happy and gay——
      And he fell in love with the Jumbly Maid
      Who came to those shores that day.
      For the Jumblies came in a Sieve, they did,
      Landing at eve near the Zemmery Fidd
      Where the oblong oysters grow,
      And the rocks are smooth and grey.

*The Jumblies all laugh out loud, as if at a joke*

Act I                                                                                           15

**Jumbly Maid** Oh Dong, you *are* funny!
**Dong** Am I? I didn't know. Yes I *am*, I'm funny, I'm funny!

*They all laugh, and go back into dumb-show*

**Narrator**   Happily, happily passed those days
While the cheerful Jumblies stayed——
They danced in circlets all night long
To the plaintive pipe of the lively Dong
In moonlight, shine or shade.
For day and night he was always there
By the side of the Jumbly Maid so fair
As on the shores they played.

*Laughter again*

**Mother** Oh Dong, we *are* going to miss you!

*The laughter suddenly stops*

**Dong** Miss me? What do you mean?

*Embarrassing silence*

**Mother** Well, when we ... go!
**Dong** Go?
**Father** Well yes, we must go sometime, you know. We still have to find the wrapper of scarlet flannel and take it back to the Pobble. I mean it's been lovely staying with you here—an undoubted treat—but sometime, you know, we'll have to pack up our things and—and go!

*Dong looks heartbroken*

**Jum** But couldn't the Dong come with us?
**Father** I'd like to say yes, nothing I'd like better, but the Sieve's not big enough for another passenger. Sorry, but there it is.
**Jumbly Maid** (*jumping up*) Then I'll stay with him!
**Father** What!
**Mother** No dear, you're far too young! And we need you with us.
**Jumbly Maid** I will. I'll stay with the Dong—I don't want him to be lonely again!
**Father** I can't possibly allow it. But I'm sure we'll meet our friend again when we've finished our quest. Yes, that's it—don't worry, Dong, one day we'll come back and see you again. That's something to look forward to, eh?

*The Dong turns away, too upset to reply, and stands apart—not looking at them*

  *The Jumblies sadly pack up and go during the next speech*

**Narrator**   Then the morning came of that hateful day
When the Jumblies sailed in their Sieve away,
And the Dong was left on the cruel shore
Gazing, gazing for evermore——
Ever keeping his weary eyes on
That pea-green sail on the far horizon.

*Dong gives a heartbroken wave*

**Dong** (*to himself*)  Goodbye, Jumblies—-goodbye, Jumbly Maid!
**Narrator**   And since that day he wanders still
By lake and forest, marsh and hill,
Playing a pipe with silvery squeaks
All day his Jumbly girl he seeks.

And because at night he could not see,
He gathered the bark of the Twangum tree
On the desolate Plain that grows——
And he wove him a wondrous nose.

*Dong "makes" and puts on a luminous nose*

A nose as strange as a nose could be!
Of vast proportions and painted red,
And tied with cords to the back of his head.

*Dong starts his search*

In a hollow rounded space it ended
With a luminous lamp within suspended,
All fenced about with a bandage stout
To prevent the wind from blowing it out.

*The Lights start to dim*

And now each night, and all night long
Over the Plains still roams the Dong
Lonely and wild, all night he goes——
The Dong with a luminous Nose!
**Dong** (*calling*)  Jumbly! Jumbly!

Act I

*The Lights go down still further*

**Narrator**  When awful silence and darkness reign
Over the Great Gromboolian Plain,
Through the long, long wintry nights;

*The sound of waves on the shore fades in*

When the angry breakers roar
As they beat on the rocky shore——
When Storm-clouds brood on the towering heights
Of the hills of the Chankly Bore——

*Lightning*

Then through the vast and gloomy dark
There moves what seems a fiery spark;
Slowly it wanders—pauses—creeps,
Anon it sparkles, flashes and leaps,
As ever onward it gleaming goes——
The Dong!—the Dong!
The Dong with a luminous Nose!

**Dong** (*calling despairingly*) JUMBLY!

*The Lights fade to a Black-out. The sound of the waves is heard in the darkness. Fade sound*

END OF ACT I

# ACT II

*During the Narrator's speech, Father, Mother, Jumbly Maid and Jum may enter and take their positions sitting on the ground, dozing*

**Narrator** The Jumblies—Part Two.

> Far and few, far and few,
> Are the lands where the Jumblies live;
> Their heads are green, and their hands are blue,
> And they went to sea in a Sieve.
>
> They sailed to the Western sea, they did,
> And then by the edge of a lake
> They carefully landed their querulous craft,
> Fastened pink ribands before and abaft,
> And tethered it to a stake.
> And in the land of Jellibolee
> They sat in the shade of a Tiggory-tree,
> And there their rest did take.

### Song: Calico Pie

**Mother** (*singing quietly*)
> Calico Drum,
> The grasshoppers come,
> Butterfly, beetle and bee——
> All over the ground
> With a hop and a bound . . .

*Father is suddenly alert*

> . . . and around and around . . .

**Father** Hush!
**Mother** What is it?
**Father** It looks like a bird.
**Jumbly Maid** Where?
**Father** By that bush.

## Act II

**Mother** What sort of bird?
**Father** I don't know; it's very large.
**Jum** There was an old man who said "Hush!
I perceive a young bird in that bush."
When they said, "Is it small?", he replied "Not at all——
It's four times as big as the bush!"
**Father** Be quiet, Jum. I think it's seen us.

*The Turkey enters*

**Turkey** Of course I've seen you—and kindly don't call me a bird. I am the Turkey who lives on the Hill. Now hurry up or you'll be late.
**Jum** Late? What for?
**Turkey** Why, the wedding, of course. You *are* the wedding guests, aren't you?
**Father** Well, I'm not sure—we didn't get an invitation.
**Turkey** How could you? We haven't sent any. I'm inviting you now, but you must hurry.
**Mother** How exciting! I do enjoy a wedding.
**Father** Yes indeed. Well, come along all of you—we mustn't keep the other guests waiting.
**Turkey** Other guests? There *are* no other guests. That's why we've been waiting for *you*.
**Jum** No guests?
**Turkey** Only the pig, and he's the best man—er, best pig. I'm pleased to see you've brought a bridesmaid.
**Jumbly Maid** Me? Oh yes, I'll gladly be a bridesmaid.
**Father** But—excuse me for asking—who is getting married?
**Turkey** Why, the Owl and the Pussy-cat, who else? Here they come now.

*The Owl and the Pussy-cat enter, followed by Piggy-wig*

Your guests have arrived at last.
**Owl** It's very nice to have some guests.
**Pussy-cat** Yes, we didn't realize the island would be almost deserted when we landed here.
**Jum** Landed—did you come in a Sieve, too?
**Owl** A Sieve? No, a boat.
**Turkey** A very beautiful boat——

**Pussy-cat**  Pea-green!

### Song: The Owl and the Pussy-cat

**Turkey** (*singing*)
> The Owl and the Pussy-cat went to sea
> In a beautiful pea-green boat,
> They took some honey, and plenty of money
> Wrapped up in a five-pound note.
> The Owl looked up at the Stars above,
> And sang to a small guitar——

**Owl**
> O lovely Pussy! O Pussy, my love,
> What a beautiful Pussy you are,
> You are,
> You are,
> What a beautiful Pussy you are!

**Turkey**
**Pussy-cat**
> Pussy said to the Owl,
> You elegant fowl!
> How charmingly sweet you sing!
> O let us be married! Too long have we tarried
> But what shall we do for a ring?
> We sailed away, for a year and a day,
> To the land where the Bong-tree grows
> And there in a wood a Piggy-wig stood
> With a ring at the end of his nose,
> His nose,
> His nose,
> With a ring at the end of his nose.

**Owl**
> Dear Pig, are you willing to sell for one shilling
> Your ring? Said the Piggy,

**Piggy-wig**  I will!
**Owl**
> So we took it away to be married next day
> By the Turkey who lives on the hill.

**Turkey, Owl**
**Pussy-cat**
**Piggy-wig**
> We dined on mince and slices of quince
> Which we ate with a runcible spoon——
> And hand in hand on the edge of the sand
> We danced by the light of the moon,
> The moon,
> The moon,
> We danced by the light of the moon!

## Act II

**Owl** Only we didn't—get married next day, I mean.
**Turkey** Because there were no guests——
**Pussy-cat** And we did so want a proper Wedding.
**Owl** So we waited——
**Pussy-cat** —for someone to come.
**Mother** But how long have you been waiting?
**Pussy-cat** Ages.
**Owl** Years and years.
**Mother** How sad!
**Turkey** Yes, but you're here now, and I can perform the ceremony. Dearly Beloved, we are gathered here—oh, but we'll skip all that ... I really feel we've waited long enough. Piggy-wig, have you got the ring? Thank you; I now pronounce you Owl and Wife. Let the wedding feast commence!
**Jum** Feast—wow!
**Owl** Well—not exactly a feast. More of a taste, really.
**Pussy-cat** Yes, there's only mince, I'm afraid. We ate all the honey while we were waiting.
**Father** No honey? Then allow me to present you with our hive of silvery bees as a wedding present. Now you can have honey whenever you want.
**Owl** Oh, thank you.
**Mother** And we've some Stilton cheese left, and half the Cranberry tart.
**Father** And I'll open the last bottle of Ring-Bo-Ree. Quiet, everybody. I'll propose a toast while they cut the cake.
**Jum** Cut the cake!
**Father** Well—slice the quince, then. To the happy couple!
**All** The happy couple!
**Father** And now we must be on our way.
**Pussy-cat** Thank you so much. If you ever have a wedding——
**Owl** —and we hope you will——
**Pussy-cat** —we'd love to be guests. Where are you going now?
**Father** To continue our search.
**Mother** We must find the scarlet wrapper.
**Jum** So the Pobble can get his toes back again.
**Jumbly Maid** But we don't know where to look
**Turkey** Why not ask the Quangle Wangle?
**Pussy-cat** Yes, he knows an awful lot of people.
**Owl** A lot of awful people!

**Turkey** Certainly many strange creatures do call on him. One of them might know what became of it.
**Father** Thank you, that's what we'll do. Goodbye.
**Owl** Goodbye. And don't forget—if you ever have a wedding——
**Pussy-cat** Be sure to invite us. Goodbye.
**Father** Goodbye. Wait—this Quangle Wangle, where does he live?
**Turkey** On top of the Crumpetty Tree, of course. Goodbye.

*Everyone exits, leaving the Narrator alone*

The Crumpetty Tree

*Up high sits the Quangle Wangle wearing an enormously wide and highly-decorated hat, his head down so that his face cannot be seen. The other creatures enter and supplicate to him when their names are mentioned*

| | |
|---|---|
| **Narrator** | On top of the Crumpetty Tree |
| | The Quangle Wangle sat, |
| | But his face you could not see |
| | On account of his Beaver Hat. |
| | For his Hat was a hundred and two feet wide, |
| | With ribbons and bibbons on every side |
| | And bells and buttons, and loops and lace, |
| | So that nobody ever could see the face |
| | Of the Qwangle Wangle Quee. |
| | |
| | And there came to the Crumpetty Tree |
| | Mr and Mrs Canary; |
| | And they said: |
| **Mr Canary** | Did you ever see |
| | Any spot so charmingly airy? |
| | May we build a nest on your lovely Hat? |
| **Mrs Canary** | Mr Quangle Wangle, grant us that! |
| | O please let us come and build a nest |
| | Of whatever material suits you best, |
| | Mr Quangle Wangle Quee! |

*Quangle Wangle signals acquiescence. Canaries arrange the scarlet wrapper on his hat*

## Act II

**Narrator**   And besides, to the Crumpetty Tree,
With a hiss and a buzz and a growl,
Came the Snake and the Bumble-Bee,
The Frog and the Fimble Fowl——
And the Blue Baboon, who played the flute,
And the Orient Calf from the land of Tute——
And the Attery Squash, and the Bisky Bat,
All came and built on the lovely Hat
Of the Quangle Wangle Quee!

*They dance*

*The Jumbly family enter*

**Jum**  Coo, look at that hat!
**Father**  Yes, a trifle vulgar I think. Ostentatious to a degree. I really feel that hats should enhance their owners' features, rather than obscure them entirely—though in some case that could be an improvement! Don't you agree, my dear?
**Mother**  I'm not sure; it certainly is—large.
**Father**  Quite—large and vulgar. Not at all the thing for persons of style.
**Jumbly Maid**  I think it's lovely.
**Father**  Yes, well, you're young. The young have no discrimination in these things. No doubt your brother agrees with you.
**Mother**  Do you, Jum?
**Jum**  (*not listening*) Do I what?
**Jumbly Maid**  Oh, you're impossible! What do you think of the Hat?
**Jum**  I think—I think that it's got a scarlet flannel wrapper on it!
**Father**  What!
**Jum**  Yes—it must be the one! Come on!
**Father**  Just a moment, a little decorum if you please. We have not been invited. We must ring the bell.

*Father rings the bell. Nobody answers; he rings again*

**Fimble Fowl**  (*to Quangle Wangle*) I beg your pardon for mentioning it, Sire, but persons are ringing on the door—I mean, knocking at the bell.
**Quangle Wangle**  (*without looking up*) I know.

*Father rings again*

**Fimble Fowl** Pardon me for disturbing you yet again, Sire, but the persons are still waiting.
**Quangle Wangle** (*as before*) Let them wait.
**Jum** Well, talk about rude!
> There was an old man who said "Well!
> Will Nobody answer this bell?
> I have pulled day and night till my hair has grown white,
> But nobody answers this bell!"

**Father** Yes, his manners certainly leave something to be desired. Vulgar, as I have already remarked.
**Jum** Well, I've had enough of this! (*Going forward*) Hey there, you with the pancake on your head, you've kept us waiting long enough! There's something on that hat that isn't yours, and we want it back!
**Father**
**Mother** } (*together*) Jum!
**Fimble fowl** I *beg* your pardon! How dare you speak to the great and gracious Quangle Wangle like that! Go away! Leave this garden at once!
**Other creatures** Yes, go on! Go away! Be off with you (*etc.*)
**Jum** Huh!
> There was an old man in a Garden
> Who always begged everyone's pardon.
> When they asked him, "What for?" he replied
> "You're a bore!
> And I *trust* you'll get out of my Garden!"

**Father** Jum, that is not the way to get it.

*Father goes forward; Jum retires*

Perhaps I could speak, your Excellency. Please excuse my son his youthful exuberance. But there is something in what he says, even if he expresses it somewhat crudely. You do indeed seem to be the receiver of stolen goods, and I'm sure that your Excellency would not wish his reputation——
**Quangle Wangle** Shut up, you old windbag!
**Father** Well, really! (*He turns away angrily*)

*Mother goes forward*

**Mother** Please sir—we have travelled a long way looking for the

## Act II

wrapper of scarlet flannel which now decorates your wonderful Hat. I'm sure whoever brought it to you didn't realize that the poor little Pobble would lose all his toes. If you would only let us return it to him then his toes might come back, and that would make him so happy. Oh, won't you help us — please!

*There is some discussion between the creatures*

**Fimble Fowl** The great and gracious Quangle Wangle finds your request touching but improperly expressed. Kindly readdress your petition in the proper manner.
**Father** Proper manner! Whatever does he mean?
**Jumbly Maid** I think I know. (*She goes forward*)
    We come to the Crumpetty Tree
    From lands both far and few.
    We have sailed the impetuous sea
    To beg a boon of you;
    From the sandy coves of Coromandel
    We have sought the wrapper of scarlet flannel
    That presently decks your wondrous Hat——
    Mr Quangle Wangle, grant us that,
    Mr Quangle Wangle Quee!

*They all wait tensely*

**Quangle Wangle** (*raising his head for the first time, so we can see that it is the Objector*) NO!
**Jumbly Family** What?!
**Quangle Wangle** Oh, all right then, since you ask so nicely. But I still think it's a stupid story!
**Jumbly Family** (*greatly relieved*) Oh, thank you.
**Quangle Wangle** Just a moment; you must give me something in return.
**Father** But we have nothing to give!
**Quangle Wangle** Nothing? What about those bottles of Ring-Bo-Ree, and all that Stilton Cheese?
**Mother** All gone, I'm afraid. We have nothing left.
**Quangle Wangle** Nothing at all?
**Jumbly Maid** We have nothing left in all the world except the Sieve.
**Quangle Wangle** Then leave me the Sieve.
**Jum** That's not fair! How can we get home without it?

**Quangle Wangle** That's your problem—the wrapper or the Sieve. Take it or leave it, that's my final offer.
**Father** Without the Sieve it will be difficult to take the wrapper home.
**Mother** Without the wrapper there's no point in going home.
**Father** Hmmm. What do you think, Jumbly Maid?
**Jumbly Maid** You *know* what I think. Jum?
**Jum** We came for the wrapper—it's no good going back without it.
**Father** Then we're all agreed. (*To Quangle Wangle*) We will accept the wrapper.
**Quangle Wangle** It's your choice.

*Fimble Fowl takes the wrapper and gives it to Father*

**Father** Thank you. We leave you the Sieve.
**Quangle Wangle** Good! Now you'll have to get back as best you can, won't you? (*Meanly*) Suddenly this story's getting better!

*Quangle Wangle exits with his retinue*

*The Torrible Zone. Lighting change or music denotes the passing of time. The Jumbly family are walking on the spot, wearily. Jum stumbles. They stop*

**Mother** Are you all right, Jum?
**Jum** I think I've twisted my ankle. Where are we?
**Father** This must be the Torrible Zone. If my calculations are correct we have to keep going north to cross the Gromboolian Plain and the hills of the Chankly Bore.
**Jumbly Maid** We'll never make it.
**Father** We must.
**Mother** But all that way without any food! Couldn't we stop and rest for a while?
**Father** The longer we take, the longer we go without food; there's nothing here.
**Mother** But we must rest.
**Jum** We can't. Dad's right—we've got to push on.
**Mother** If we don't stop we might die of exhaustion!
**Jum** If we do stop, we might starve to death before we find anything to eat.
**Jumbly Maid** He's right, Mother—we've got to keep going.

Act II 27

**Father** That's agreed, then, on we go.
**Mother** But Jum's ankle . . .?
**Jum** It's all right, Mum, I'll manage. Let's get going.

*They resume walking on the spot, and continue during the next speech*

**Narrator** For days and days they staggered on
Until their feet were sore.
Hungry and tired and entirely alone,
They travelled the wastes of the Torrible Zone
To an unfamiliar shore.
The purpledicular crags they crossed
Until at last, completely lost,
They just could walk no more.

*The Great Gromboolian Plain. Night*

**Mother** Stop a minute.

*They stop*

**Jumbly Maid** What's the matter?
**Mother** Day after day, week after week, we've been walking—how long must we carry on?
**Jum** Until we get there.
**Mother** But when will that be—Father?
**Father** Well, of course we have no means of knowing, but I should think——
**Mother** Do you know where we are? Have you any idea where we're going?
**Father** Well, not exactly, no. We might be in the middle of the Great Gromboolian Plain, but then again——
**Mother** Yes?
**Father** —we might not.
**Mother** In other words, we're lost?
**Father** (*defeatedly*) Yes.
**Jum** But if we keep going north——
**Mother** How do we know which is north? We can tell by the sun during the day, but tonight there isn't one star in the sky. Stumbling over rocks and into bushes—we could be going round in circles! And who knows what might be lurking in the dark!

**Jumbly Maid** (*screaming*) Ugh!
**Father** What is it?
**Jumbly Maid** I just stood on something soft and squashy!
**Jum** That was my foot!
**Jumbly Maid** (*relieved*) Oh, that's all right, then.
**Jum** It might be all right for you——
**Father** Stop it, you two. Now let's hold hands and press on.
**Mother** If only it wasn't so dark!
**Jum** There was a young man in the dark,
Who thought he could see a small spark——
**Father** Be quiet, Jum; this is no time for your stupid rhymes.
**Jum** But I can, I *can* see a small spark. Look!
**Mother** Where?
**Jum** Over there.
**Jumbly Maid** I can see it now—moving backwards and forwards almost as if it's searching for something. Whatever can it be?
**Father** Whatever it is, I rather fear it might be searching for *us*. Keep very still.
**Dong** (*off, calling from afar*) Jumblies!
**Jum** It *is* searching for us. But what——?
**Jumbly Maid** (*jumping up*) I know!
**Father** Get down! Have you gone mad? You have no idea——
**Jumbly Maid** But I have! I know who it is! (*Calling*) Here! We're over here!
**Dong** (*off, nearer*) Jumblies!
**All** It's the Dong!

*Dong enters, his nose illuminated*

**Dong** The Jumblies—at last!
**Jum** Good old Dong!
**Father** My dear fellow—but what's happened to your nose?
**Dong** Never mind that now, it's a long story. The point is, it worked. All this time I've been searching for you, and now I've found you—thanks to my luminous nose! But what are you doing in the middle of the Great Gromboolian Plain? And where is your Sieve?
**Father** That, too, is a long story. We've lost our Sieve, but we *have* got the wrapper of scarlet flannel!
**Mother** And now we're trying to get back home with it. The poor

## Act II

little Pobble will be so anxious. But it *is* such a pleasure to see you again, (*to Jumbly Maid*) isn't it, dear?
**Jumbly Maid** It certainly is.
**Father** However, that doesn't solve the problem of how to find our way home.
**Dong** But I could guide you!
**Jum** Could you?
**Dong** (*excitedly*) Of course I could! I have wandered this Plain day and night for years. I know it like the back of my hand. I could take you across the Plain, over the hills of the Chankly Bore and all the way home! (*Suddenly embarrassed*) Er, that is—if you'd like me to.
**Jum** Would we? Wow—you bet!
**Father** We'd like nothing better. Now that we're not travelling in the Sieve, there's no reason why you shouldn't join us permanently.
**Mother** Yes, come and live with us in Coromandel. We'd all like that, wouldn't we, Jumbly Maid?
**Jumbly Maid** (*shyly*) I'd like that very much.
**Jum** What are we waiting for? It's back to Coromandel ... Yippee!!

*Holding hands and with the Dong leading, they dance off to the Coromandel tune, which continues into the next scene*

*Coromandel*

*Jumblies—but not the family—dance in and frolic to the Coromandel tune, which may be sung if required. The Pobble wanders among them, sad and isolated. They exit, leaving the Pobble gazing out to sea*

### Far and Few

**Pobble** (*singing mournfully*)
    Far and few, far and few,
    Are the lands where the Jumblies live;
    Their heads are green, and their hands are blue,
    And they went to sea in a sieve!

*A Jumbly Woman and Child enter*

**Child** Mummy, who's that?

**Woman** That's the Pobble, dear. Don't stare at him—it's rude.
**Child** What's he singing about? Who went to sea in a Sieve?
**Woman** Hush, dear. We don't talk about it. It all happened a long time ago.
**Child** Mummy, why hasn't he got any toes?
**Woman** Don't ask so many questions; come on!

*The Woman and Child exit*

*The Pobble sings again*

*Aunt Jobiska enters*

**Aunt Jobiska** You'll wear your eyes out, Pobble, you really will—gazing out to sea all the time. Why don't you come down and join in the fun?
**Pobble** They'll come back, Aunt Jobiska, I know they will. One day they'll appear on the horizon waving my wrapper of scarlet flannel, and my toes will be restored. What did Jumbly say all those years ago—"Lost all hope!" ... I'll never lose hope. They *will* come back.
**Aunt Jobiska** Perhaps. But it's getting dark now and they're just starting to cook the oysters. Let's go down and join them.
**Pobble** You go, Aunt Jobiska, I'll come down later. I think I'll wait just a little longer.
**Aunt Jobiska** (*starting to go*) Well, don't be too long, dear. And don't keep singing that song—you know it upsets the others.
**Pobble** (*excitedly*) Wait, Aunt, I think I see them! Yes! yes! They're here! Come quickly, everyone—the Jumblies have come back!

*All Jumblies rush in and welcome the travellers, who enter with the Dong*

**All** They're back, the Jumblies are back! (*Etc.*)
**1st Jumbly** They've got taller!
**2nd Jumbly** They've got thinner!
**3rd Jumbly** They've got older!
**4th Jumbly** They've got wiser!
**5th Jumbly** They've got a friend with a funny nose!

*The travellers are swept along by the welcome, and take positions for a feast. The Pobble is rather forgotten in all this*

## Act II

**Narrator** And in twenty years they all came back,
In twenty years or more——
And everyone said, "How tall they've grown!
For they've been to the Lakes, and the Torrible Zone,
And the hills of the Chankly Bore!"
And they drank their health, and gave them a feast
Of dumplings made of beautiful yeast,
And oblong oysters, fresh from the sea,
And dozens of glasses of Ring-Bo-Ree,
Till they could eat no more.

**Father** Fellow Jumblies, it's wonderful to see you all again! As you know, I'm not one to make a speech, but this reminds me of that fateful day twenty years ago when we stood on this very shore ready to embark on our perilous mission. Little did we know then, what adventures lay in wait for us in those far-off lands as we——

**Jum** Dad! Get on with it.

**Father** Yes, quite. Well, you will have noticed an unfamiliar face amongst us. This is our good friend the Dong, who has been such a help in times of trouble. I'm sure you'll make him most welcome, especially when I tell you that he is to marry my daughter——

**Mother** *Our* daughter, dear.

**Father** Yes, of course, dear – our daughter, the Jumbly Maid!

**All** Hooray!

**Father** Thank you, thank you. (*To Jumbly Maid*) Would you like to say a word, my dear?

**Jumbly Maid** Just to thank you all for your kind thoughts, and to say how much I'm looking forward to being a Bride.

*She glances shyly at Dong, who is suitably embarrassed*

I have already been a bridesmaid, and I only wish the Owl and the Pussy-cat could be here as *our* guests.

*The Owl and Pussy-cat enter, followed by Turkey and Piggy-wig*

**Owl** But we *are* here!

**Pussy-cat** We came as soon as we heard.

**Owl** We wouldn't want to miss *your* wedding——

**Pussy-cat** Not for the world!

**Turkey** And I would deem it a great honour to conduct the ceremony.
**Father** Of course you must. Isn't this wonderful!
**Owl** And look who we met on the way——
**Pussy-cat** —so we invited them along.

*The Pelicans enter*

**Mother** Your Majesty—what an honour!
**Pelican King** Ploffskin, Pluffskin, the pleasure is mine.
**Pelicans** Mine, mine, mine, mine, mine!
**Father** Well, well, well, what a delightful homecoming it has been. Now everyone is here!
**Mother** Except the Quangle Wangle.
**Jum** Huh, *him*!
**Father** Well I hardly think we should invite *him* to our celebrations.
**Mother** Oh, I don't know—forgive and forget. What do you think, Jumbly Maid?
**Jumbly Maid** Leave it to me.
        Come down from your Crumpetty Tree
        To the lands both far and few,
        Where we sing and dance with glee,
        And we beg that you will too.
        O please descend from your lofty station
        To come and join in our celebration,
        Delighting us all with your wondrous Hat;
        Mr Quangle Wangle, grant us that,
        Mr Quangle Wangle Quee!

*Quangle Wangle and his retinue enter*

**Quangle Wangle** Thanks for including me—perhaps it wasn't such a bad story after all!
**All** Hooray!
**Jum** (*urgently*) Dad, Dad! What about the Pobble?
**Father** Goodness me, we're forgetting the whole purpose for our voyage! Young Pobble, step forward.

*Pobble is brought forward*

**Father** Fellow Jumblies and friends; twenty years ago we set off

Act II                                                                    33

from these shores to seek the wrapper of scarlet flannel. You will be pleased to hear that we have been successful!

*Cheers*

But none so pleased, I imagine, as our good friend the Pobble. Jum, you found this young fellow in the first place, so I think you should be the one. Come on.

*Applause as Jum steps forward with the wrapper*

**Jum** Here you are, Pobble. (*He wraps it round him*) Gosh, I hope it works!
**Father** It has! His toes have been restored!
**All** Hooray!
**Jumbly Maid** Oh, Father! Have they really come back?
**Father** Yes! Twenty-six toes to each leg, and that's no mean feat! —just my little joke, you understand!

*The others groan*

**Pobble** Oh thank you, thank you all! Look, Aunt Jobiska, *I've got toes*!
**Narrator** The Pobble who had no toes
Is now as happy as we.
His toes are restored, and so never more
Will he say "Fish fiddle de-dee!"
And his Aunt Jobiska cooked them a dish
Of eggs and buttercups fried with fish,
And she said:
**Aunt Jobiska** It's a fact the whole world knows,
That Pobbles are happier *with* their toes!

### Song: The Coast of Coromandel

**All** On the Coast of Coromandel
Where the bong trees softly sway,
There we play the festive mandolin
And frolic all the day.
And at night we gently snore
On that Coromandel shore,
For we'll go to sea no more——
Never ever any more!

(*Repeat*)

### Song: Far and Few

Far and few, far and few,
Are the lands where the Jumblies live;
Their heads are green, and their hands are blue,
And they went to sea in a Sieve.

THE END

## THE COAST OF COROMANDEL

A LIVELY DANCE

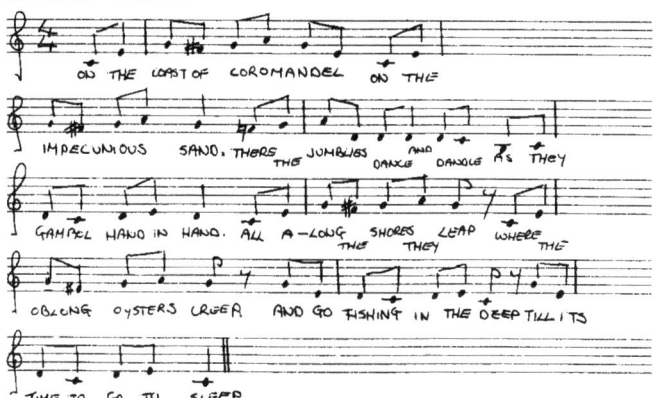

1. On the Coast of Coromandel
   On the impecunious sand,
   There the Jumblies dance and dandle
   As they gambol hand in hand.
   All along the shores they leap,
   Where the oblong oysters creep,
   And go fishing in the deep
   Till it's time to go to sleep.

2. A large Sieve without a handle
   They employ without delay
   On that Coast of Coromandel
   Where the Bong trees softly sway;
   Crooning songs evocative
   To the oysters where they live
   While they catch them in the Sieve,
   Gently catch them in the Sieve.

3. On the Coast of Coromandel
   Next the superincumbent sea,
   By the light of half a candle
   They prepare to cook their tea——
   And the oblong oysters roast
   With a slice of scroobious toast
   On that Coromandel Coast,
   Dreamy Coromandel Coast.

4. On the Coast of Coromandel
   Where the Bong trees softly sway,
   There we play the festive mandolin
   And frolic all the day.
   And at night we gently snore
   On that Coromandel shore,
   For we'll go to sea no more——
   Never ever any more!

# The Voyage of the Jumblies

## CALICO PIE

SLOWLY AND DREAMILY: A LULLABY

1. Calico Pie,
   The little birds fly,
   Down to the Calico Tree——
   Their wings were blue,
   And they sang "Tilly-loo"
   Till away they flew
   And they never came back to me.

   > They never came back,
   > They never came back——
   > They never came back to me.

2. Calico Jam,
   The little fish swam
   Down to the Calico Sea——

He took off his hat
To the sole and the sprat,
And the Willeby-wat,
But they never came back to me.

> They never came back,
> They never came back——
> They never came back to me.

3. Calico Drum,
    The grasshoppers come,
    Butterfly, beetle and bee——
    All over the ground
    With a hop and a bound ...
    ... and around and around ...

The Voyage of the Jumblies

## THE PELICAN CHORUS

JERKILY, NOT TOO FAST.

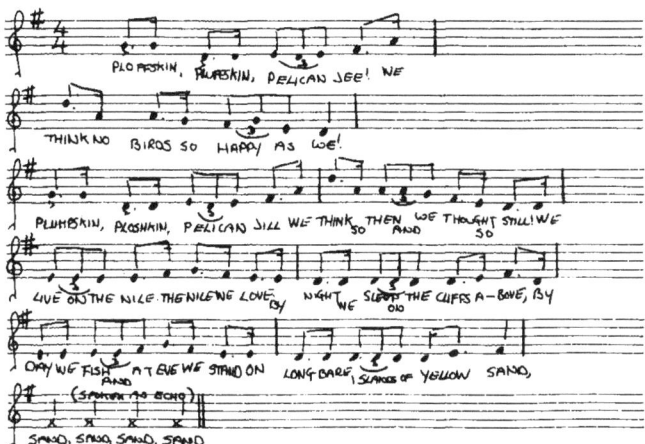

    (*Chorus*)  Ploffskin, Pluffskin, Pelican Jee!
                We think no birds so happy as we!
                Plumpskin, Ploshkin, Pelican Jill——
                We think so then and we thought so still!

1. We live on the Nile. The Nile we love.
   By night we sleep on the cliffs above;
   By day we fish, and at eve we stand
   On long bare islands of yellow sand,
   (Sand, sand, sand, sand)

   (*Chorus*) Ploffskin, Pluffskin, etc.

2. And when the sun sinks slowly down
   And the great rock walls grow dark and brown,
   The purple river rolls fast and dim
   And the ivory ibis starlike skim,
   (Skim, skim, skim, skim)

   (*Chorus*) Ploffskin, Pluffskin, etc.

3. Then wing to wing we dance around
   Stamping our feet with a flumpy sound,
   Clashing our beaks as Pelicans ought,
   And this is the song we nightly snort,
   (Snort, snort, snort, snort)

   (*Chorus*) Ploffskin, Pluffskin, etc.

The Voyage of the Jumblies 41

## THE OWL AND THE PUSSYCAT

1. The Owl and the Pussy-cat went to sea
   In a beautiful pea-green boat.
   They took some honey and plenty of money
   Wrapped up in a five-pound note.
   The Owl looked up at the stars above,
   And sang to a small guitar ---
   O lovely Pussy! O Pussy my love
   What a beautiful Pussy you are, you are, you are,
   What a beautiful Pussy you are!

2. Pussy said to the Owl, "you elegant fowl!
   How charmingly sweet you sing!
   O let us be married! Too long have we tarried
   But what shall we do for a ring?"

We sailed away, for a year and a day,
To the land where the bong-tree grows
And there in a wood a Piggy-wig stood
With a ring at the end of this nose, his nose, his nose,
With a ring at the end of his nose.

3. "Dear Pig, are you willing to sell for one shilling
Your ring?"—said the Piggy "I will!"
So we took it away to be married next day
By the Turkey who lives on the hill.
We dined on mince and slices of quince
Which we ate with a runcible spoon——
And hand in hand on the edge of the sand
We danced by the light of the moon, the moon, the moon,
We danced by the light of the moon!

# The Voyage of the Jumblies

Far and few, far and few,
Are the lands where the Jumblies live;
Their heads are green, and their hands are blue,
And they went to sea in a Sieve.

"Far and Few" is mostly recited to form part of the narration, but on two occasions it is sung—mournfully by the Pobble in Act II, majestically by the whole cast to end the play.

# LIGHTING PLOT

Property fittings required: nil

ACT I

*To open:* Full general lighting

| Cue 1 | **Narrator:** "... To prevent the wind from blowing it out."<br>*Gradually dim lighting* | (Page 16) |
| Cue 2 | **Dong:** "Jumbly! Jumbly!"<br>*Dim lighting further* | (Page 16) |
| Cue 3 | **Narrator:** "... Of the hills of Chankly Bore——"<br>*Lightning* | (Page 17) |
| Cue 4 | **Dong:** "JUMBLY!"<br>*Fade to black-out* | (Page 17) |

ACT II

*To open:* Full general lighting

| Cue 5* | **Quangle Wangle** exits with his retinue<br>*Dim lighting slightly* | (Page 26) |
| Cue 6 | **Narrator:** "... they just could walk no more."<br>*Dim to night effect* | (Page 27) |
| Cue 7 | The **Jumblies** and **Dong** exit dancing<br>*Bring up full general lighting* | (Page 29) |

*Cue 5 is optional and music may be substituted to indicate the passing of time

# EFFECTS PLOT

## ACT I

*Cue* 1   **Narrator:** "... through the long, long wintry nights ..."   (Page 17)
*Fade in sound of waves on the seashore; continue*

*Cue* 2   The Lights fade to Black-out   (Page 17)
*Pause, then fade sound of waves*

## ACT II

*No cues*

www.ingramcontent.com/pod-product-compliance
Ingram Content Group UK Ltd.
Pitfield, Milton Keynes, MK11 3LW, UK
UKHW021848210426
5322IPUK00022B/535